INTROD...

Walter
Benja...

Howard Caygill, Alex Coles and Andrzej Klimowski

with Richard Appignanesi

ICON BOOKS UK   TOTEM BOOKS USA

This edition published in the UK in 2000 by Icon Books Ltd., Grange Road, Duxford, Cambridge CB2 4QF
email: info@iconbooks.co.uk
www.iconbooks.co.uk

Distributed in the UK, Europe, Canada, South Africa and Asia by the Penguin Group: Penguin Books Ltd., 27 Wrights Lane, London W8 5TZ

This edition published in Australia in 2000 by Allen & Unwin Pty. Ltd., PO Box 8500, 9 Atchison Street, St. Leonards NSW 2065

Previously published in the UK and Australia in 1998 under the title
Walter Benjamin for Beginners

First published in the United States in 1998 by Totem Books

In the United States, distributed to the trade by National Book Network Inc., 4720 Boston Way, Lanham, Maryland 20706

Library of Congress catalog card number applied for

Originating editor: Richard Appignanesi

Printed and bound in Australia
by McPherson's Printing Group, Victoria

Walter Benjamin eludes classification. He seemed content with the name "critic". But an exceptional critic of such passion, erudition and virtuosity who transforms the nature of what usually passes for criticism. His gaze is multiple: philosophy, language, art, architecture, photography, history, Jewish mysticism, Marxism. He does not merely glance at these but digs to their foundations.

EVERY IMAGE OF THE PAST THAT IS NOT RECOGNIZED BY THE PRESENT AS ONE OF ITS OWN CONCERNS THREATENS TO DISAPPEAR IRRETRIEVABLY.

If this book can help the reader through the dazzling maze of Benjamin's work, it will be at the end to find Benjamin the *allegorist*.

SNAPSHOTS OF A BERLIN CHILDHOOD

Walter Benjamin was born 15 July 1892 in Berlin. His parents were Emil, a businessman, and his wife Pauline, née Schönflies. They were Jewish, unassimilated to Christianity, but like many others not strictly observant.

He remembered his childhood experiences in a series of memoirs written when he was contemplating suicide in 1932, "Berlin Chronicle" and "A Berlin Childhood Around 1900". The hybrid nature of these texts – at once cultural criticism and personal reflection – exemplifies the complexity of Benjamin's writings which transgress disciplinary borders and rules of genre.

Benjamin presents his memories in the form of snapshot mosaic images, a practice which anticipates his later comments on the philosophy of history. He remembered himself walking reluctantly half a step behind his mother while out shopping.

In another image Benjamin remembered seeing a sandwich man vainly trying to give away leaflets.

He recalled with particular pleasure reading the latest edition of the *New Companion to German Youth* with its hunting and spy stories which he read illicitly under the bed-covers at night.

Many of these recollected images are tinged with a sense of catastrophe and desperation, such as the flood disaster which left the young Benjamin abandoned on the main shopping boulevard of Berlin, the Kurfürstendamm.

I FELT PARTICULARLY EXPOSED TO THE ELEMENTAL POWER OF NATURE WHICH MADE THE CITY SEEM LIKE A PRIMEVAL FOREST

While composing his memoirs, Benjamin was partial to hashish and some images show the influence of this: such as his recollection of the Berlin victory column in the park, associated with the words: "O brown-baked column of victory/with children's sugar from the winter days." Death haunts these images.

MY FATHER ENTERED MY BEDROOM AT NIGHT WITH NEWS OF A RELATIVE'S DEATH. HE USED A STRANGE WORD THAT I FORGOT. "SYPHILIS".

Here we find an example of Benjamin's characteristic insight: the manifestation of death "in little things".

For all of his life, Benjamin carried with him a horror and fascination for the luxuriously appointed bourgeois interior – the over-furnished drawing-room.

Although affluent, these interiors were not comfortable. As Benjamin said, "They had no space for dying – which is why their owners died in a sanatorium, while the furniture went straight to the second-hand dealer."

Benjamin's encounter with art began early, with him posing for individual and family photographs.

This was particularly difficult when he had to pose in front of a crudely painted backdrop of the Alps, holding a walking stick, bareheaded, sporty, and gazing into the distance with a tortured smile on his lips.

The magnitude of his torments at home and at the photographer's studio faded before those of school. He attended the Kaiser Friedrich School in Berlin's wealthy Charlottenberg west-end, where he enjoyed a relatively privileged education. The name of the school reflected the attitudes of the staff and the content of the curriculum. The ethos of the German Imperial Army was ever-present, along with a commitment to unremitting industry: "If I rest, I rust." The teachers were a strange crew of Imperial parodies who did not recognize the future brilliance of their pupil. They found him "well-behaved but with inadequate handwriting".

Benjamin's horror of the discipline of school – its routines, rituals and daily humiliation – moved his parents to send him for two years to an experimental school in the country at the age of 14. At the Haubinda school in Thuringia, Benjamin was taught by the educational reformer Gustav Wyneken.

Wyneken introduced Benjamin to the blossoming Youth Movement in Germany which consisted of various separate groups and organizations of young people.

These ranged from clubs of hikers and ramblers to vaguely anarchistic groups such as the one Wyneken encouraged Benjamin to join. But there were also anti-Semitic and proto-Nazi bands, for example the Youth League of the Imperial Faithful. Benjamin became a teenage rebel, travelling the country giving lectures and writing in the youth fanzines on the need for the young to follow their own inclinations.

THE PERIPATETIC PHILOSOPHY STUDENT

Like many German students then and now, Benjamin attended a number of different universities. He left the Kaiser Friedrich School with good results in literature but a weakness in mathematics, and undertook an extended journey to Italy. In 1912, at the age of 20, he enrolled to study philosophy at the University of Freiburg in Bresgau. He attended lectures by the neo-Kantian philosopher **Heinrich Rickert** (1863-1936) which he found extremely boring.

SCIENCE CAN ONLY ESTABLISH CONCEPTUAL **CLARITY** ON THE **PLURALITY** OF WORLD-VIEWS PRESENT IN ACTUALITY AND THUS BECOME THE **DOCTRINE** OF WORLD-VIEWS.

While suffering in the back row, he penned a short poem for his friend Herbert Belmore: "Science is a cow/I listen/I sit in the lecture hall/while it goes moo."

Also in the audience was another student philosopher, **Martin Heidegger** (1889-1976). There is no record of them having met or spoken to each other, although Benjamin's later comments on Heidegger are far from complimentary.

Heidegger did not ever mention Benjamin in any of his works or reflections.

From 1912 to 1915, Benjamin carried on a peripatetic study of philosophy at the universities of Freiburg, Berlin and Munich. Apart from these studies, he also attended courses in art and literary history, as well as others in Berlin by the influential sociologist and cultural historian **Georg Simmel** (1858-1918).

It was from Simmel that Benjamin gained his fascination with modern urban experience.

In 1915, Benjamin attended courses at the University of Munich by **Heinrich Wölfflin** (1864-1945), the great art historian and specialist in Baroque art. Benjamin was not impressed. "A by no means overwhelmingly gifted man, who, by nature, has no more feel for art than anyone else, but who attempts to get around this by using all the energy and resources of his personality (which have nothing to do with art)."

Benjamin's hostility to Wölfflin is interesting in the light of his own interest in art and in the Baroque age, as we'll see later.

KANT AND NEO-KANTIANISM

The kind of philosophy studied at the time by Benjamin was known as neo-Kantianism, a late 19th century development of Kant's theory of knowledge. **Immanuel Kant** (1724-1804) had severely undermined metaphysics' pretensions to **transcendent** knowledge in his *Critique of Pure Reason* (1781). The concept of the soul, for example, is transcendent: it is an unobservable substance, and as such, unknowable by our minds which depend on the raw material of sense-data. But there is a difference between transcendent and the **transcendental.**

THE TRANSCENDENTAL IS THE LOGICAL APPARATUS OF CONCEPTS, COMMON TO ALL MINDS, WHICH ORGANIZES **EXPERIENCE** AND IS THUS LOGICALLY PRIOR TO IT.

Concepts are **logically prior**, Kant says. And it is this aspect, after the critical failure of metaphysics, that the neo-Kantians fastened on in developing their theory of knowledge, named **apriorism** or **aprioristic epistemology**. Apriorism, as the opposite of empiricism, believes there is substantial knowledge possible which does not depend on experience for its justification: for instance, "every event has a cause". But, of course, such a *priori* knowledge is still metaphysical.

Benjamin developed his own version of radical neo-Kantianism, as we'll see.

PHENOMENOLOGY

Benjamin also encountered the emergent school of Phenomenology as elaborated by **Edmund Husserl** (1859-1938). This method of descriptive psychology was a further extension of apriorism, an investigation of the logical elements in thought that are common to all minds.

During these years of peripatetic academic studies, Benjamin also pursued his engagement with the Youth Movement. He served on the organizing committees of the Berlin Youth Movement and gave a number of lectures to and about youth.

We see him bringing together his commitment to youth and his studies in an attempt to write the philosophy of the Youth Movement.

Benjamin used the vocabulary of neo-Kantianism but applied it to the ends of the theoretical debate within the Youth Movement. In texts such as "The Metaphysics of Youth" (1913-14) and "Student Life" (1915), Benjamin elaborated an original and idiosyncratic philosophical position regarding historical time, experience and aesthetics that supplied the foundation for his subsequent work. This philosophy was at once extremely abstract and also tied to concrete experiences, such as writing a diary.

In many respects, his early writings anticipate what was to come later, as in such phrases as: "All future is past. The past of things is the future of the 'I' time. But past things have futurity."

THINGS PERCEIVE US; THEIR GAZE PROPELS US INTO THE FUTURE, SINCE WE DO NOT RESPOND TO THEM BUT INSTEAD STEP AMONG THEM....
WE ARE THEIR FUTURE.

PRO- OR ANTI-ZIONISM?

On the eve of the First World War, the Youth Movement was becoming increasingly splintered into liberal, nationalistic and proto-fascist wings. For this reason, the status of the contribution of Jewish members was being hotly debated. In fact, the debates within Judaism itself, generally between assimilation and Zionism, were being replicated at the different levels of the Youth Movement. Already in the summer of 1912, Benjamin was arguing Zionism on the beach with his friend Kurt Tuchler in daily, one might say hourly, conversations.

Benjamin was not an enthusiastic supporter of the liberal assimilationist wing of Judaism, which either regarded Judaism as a "Sunday religion" or recommended that Jews conform to the national community by becoming Christians. But neither was he entirely convinced of the Zionist cause initiated by the pioneering zealot **Theodor Herzl** (1860-1904).

"WHAT WERE YOU DOING ON 4 AUGUST 1914?"

In Berlin, outside the bohemian Café des Westens, Benjamin looks at his watch. "At that time, I did not yet possess that passion for waiting without which one cannot thoroughly appreciate the charm of a café." In Paris, **Marcel Proust** (1871-1922) goes to bed early that night. In Prague, **Franz Kafka** (1883-1924) writes in his diary: "War started, went swimming." In Vienna, **Adolf Hitler** (1889-1945) exults at the news of war, as recorded in *Mein Kampf*.

The outbreak of the First World War spelt the end of the Youth Movement. The members of its nationalist wing were delighted, enlisted immediately, and left for the front.

The more liberal members of the Youth Movement were initially indifferent but became increasingly hostile as their adult models, Wyneken, Simmel and many others, disgraced themselves with idealistic proclamations in support of the German war for "culture" against the materialistic "civilization" of the British and the French. Benjamin's own experience of the early days of the war was coloured by the catastrophic event of the dual protest suicides of his friends, the poet Fritz Heinle and Rika Seligson.

BETRAYAL AND REVOLUTION

To appreciate Benjamin's development requires a sense of the political climate in Germany before and after the First World War. Marxists and other socialists had formed the Social-Democratic Party in 1875. It became the fastest-growing workers' party in the world and gained many seats in parliament. Socialists everywhere looked up to the German SDP as the model party of the *Second Socialist International*, founded in 1889 (the First, 1864-72, had been created by Marx and others). This international ideal of working-class solidarity collapsed in 1914 when socialists in Germany, France, Belgium and elsewhere rushed to the defence of their countries.

INTERNATIONALISM HAS COLLAPSED INTO HOSTILE NATIONALISMS!

V.I. Lenin (1870-1924), leader of the Bolshevik wing of Russian Social-Democracy, was among those Marxists, outraged by the betrayal, who now aimed to turn the crisis into a *revolution*.

Lenin in fact achieved that aim in Russia with the Bolsheviks' October Revolution, 1917, and the foundation of international Communism. The defeat of Imperial Germany in 1918 inspired attempts to imitate Lenin's "soviets" in Bavaria, Bremen, Kiel and Berlin. These were brutally suppressed by an alliance of conservative Social-Democrats, the army and right-wing militias. The Weimar Republic, created in 1919 by this Social-Democratic "betrayal", would satisfy neither leftists, Communists nor the extreme nationalist right which brought Hitler to power in 1933.

Hyper-inflation was the most serious of the Weimar Republic's persistent

social and political crises. One German mark on the price index of 1913 equalled *1,261 thousand million* marks by 1923!

HOW TO AVOID CONSCRIPTION

Benjamin sustained a principled opposition to the war for its duration, which translated itself into a series of bizarre comic attempts to avoid conscription.

At the call-up of his age group in 1914, Benjamin presented himself as a palsy victim.

On the night of 20 October 1915, preceding his medical re-examination, he stayed up all night drinking vast quantities of black coffee, so as to appear unfit next morning.

On 28 December 1916, he was classified as fit and ordered to report for field duty on 8 January 1917. His fiancée, Dora Pollak, tried another method of rescue.

Benjamin had met Dora in the Berlin intellectual milieu. They were married 17 April 1917 and their son Stefan was born 11 April 1918. Benjamin and Dora left for neutral Switzerland in 1917 where he enrolled at the University of Bern to pursue doctoral research into Kant and Romanticism.

This work can be better understood if we first consider a series of important fragments that Benjamin wrote in the summer of 1916 under the stimulus of his new friendship with **Gershom Scholem** (1897-1982), a pioneering scholar of Jewish mysticism.

FRIENDSHIP WITH GERSHOM SCHOLEM

Scholem reflected on his friendship with Benjamin in a series of memoirs: *The Story of a Friendship*. Scholem had first met Benjamin in 1915 at a meeting of the Youth Movement and the Zionist Youth Organization in Berlin. Eighty young people had gathered to discuss the relationship between their German and Jewish heritages. Scholem did not remember the contents of Benjamin's very tortuous speech, but only his peculiar manner of public speaking.

WITHOUT LOOKING AT THE AUDIENCE, HE DELIVERED HIS ABSOLUTELY LETTER-PERFECT SPEECH WITH GREAT INTENSITY TO AN UPPER CORNER OF THE CEILING, AT WHICH HE STARED THE WHOLE TIME.

Scholem had colluded with Dora in the fantastic efforts to get Benjamin declared unfit for service, and the three became close companions. Scholem followed them to Switzerland in May 1918 and found himself witness to the unhappy vagaries of Benjamin's married life with Dora.

DORA WAS EXTREMELY SOCIABLE AND VIVACIOUS— THE ANTITHESIS OF WALTER.

I'VE MET THE PHILOSOPHER ERNST BLOCH AND THE DADAIST IMPRESARIO TRISTAN TZARA HERE IN BERN, BUT...

BUT— HE'S MOSTLY DEVOTED TO SOLITARY SCHOLARSHIP!

Scholem and Benjamin developed an extremely fruitful and mutually beneficial intellectual friendship which they preserved until Benjamin's death – in the later phase through a celebrated correspondence.

Although Scholem was initially close to the Zionists, his position was sufficiently ambivalent to allow for common ground with Benjamin. Both were critical of the leading Jewish intellectual **Martin Buber** (1878-1965), Professor of Religions at Frankfurt until 1933, then from 1938, Professor of Social Philosophy in Jerusalem.

Benjamin's feelings were aired when he was invited to contribute to Buber's journal *Der Jude*, which devoted itself to Jewish and Zionist concerns.

The stimulating effects of the early stages of Benjamin's intellectual friendship with Scholem are evident in a series of fragments from the summer of 1916.

The most important are the two fragments on the dramatic forms of Tragedy and Mourning Play (*Trauerspiel*). Tragedy was the drama of ancient Greece, characterized by the unity of time, place and action. Instead, the 17th century German Mourning Play is modern in that it is characterized by **dis**unity. We can highlight the difference by considering examples of tragedy and *Trauerspiel*.

GREEK TRAGEDY

Greek drama is like a magic circle in which the hero's entire existence appears tragically fulfilled in one time, place and action. Time is conclusively shaped by the form of the drama itself. The individual's life, and hence his fate, is encapsulated at every point by the dramatic language. For instance, the life of Oedipus is already previewed in his famous reply to the Sphinx's riddle.

TRAUERSPIEL OR MOURNING PLAY

Not so with the Mourning Play. It is allegorical. The idea of a resolution exceeds the boundaries of form and dramatic time comes closer to **musical** time. The archetypal Mourning Play for Benjamin is Shakespeare's *Hamlet*, a play of ambiguity, intrigue and delay which ends in catastrophe.

The problematic character of the Mourning Play will be further developed in *The Origin of German Tragic Drama* (1928).

ON LANGUAGE

The final 1916 fragment, "On Language as Such and on the Language of Mankind", presents an original philosophy of language in the guise of a commentary on the story of the Fall and the Book of Genesis.

In it, Benjamin models experience in general on the experience of translation between languages: in this case between human, divine and the language of things.

Benjamin's exploration of language owes a great deal to an earlier criticism of Kant, the linguistic "meta-critique" of **Georg Hamann** (1730-88).

Kant in his *Critique of Pure Reason* had supposed that experience was the outcome of a fusion of spatio-temporal intuitions and the four categories of the understanding.

Georg Hamann, an acquaintance of Kant, sharply criticized the *Critique of Pure Reason* by pointing out that it overlooked the obvious role of language. "Not only the entire capacity to think rests on language, but language is also the centre of the misunderstanding of reason with itself."

Benjamin's critique of Kant did not rest at the level of Hamann's linguistic meta-critique but was taken further in his essay "The Programme of the Coming Philosophy" (1918). Benjamin criticizes Kant for basing his concept of experience on the model of mathematical and scientific experience. He argues instead that experience should be extended to include art and religious experience.

Benjamin was proposing an experience of the *absolute* to enrich Kantian critical philosophy, in effect, by retaining the possibility of metaphysics. Although this is in many ways very un-Kantian, he regarded it as feasible within the limits of Kantian philosophy.

THE EXPERIENCE OF FREEDOM

Benjamin also looked to the possibility of a new relationship between the "theory of experience and the theory of freedom". According to Kant in the *Critique of Judgement* (1790), it is in the nature of experience that Imagination can never identify with Reason and the idea of freedom.

THE EXPERIENCE OF COLOUR

The fragments from 1916 on the philosophy of language are justly celebrated but should not be allowed to overcast another series of contemporary fragments on the philosophy of colour. In 1915, Benjamin wrote "Dialogue on the Rainbow" in which he had already developed a philosophy of experience based on the experience of colour.

COLOUR DOES NOT HAVE A FIXED VALUE, BUT VARIES WITH RESPECT TO THE COLOURS THAT SURROUND IT.

This was another aspect of Benjamin's critique of Kant.

By positing the continuity of colour, Benjamin replaces two of Kant's distinctions: (1) between sensibility and the understanding (the understanding gives form to the spatio-temporal matter of sensation) and (2) between a subject and an object of knowledge.

I TOO WAS NOT, NOR MY UNDERSTANDING, THAT RESOLVES THINGS OUT OF THE IMAGES OF THE SENSES. I WAS NOT THE ONE WHO SAW, BUT ONLY SEEING. AND WHAT I SAW WERE NOT THINGS ... BUT ONLY COLOURS. AND I TOO WAS COLOURED INTO THIS LANDSCAPE.

GERMAN ROMANTIC ART CRITICISM

Benjamin's doctoral dissertation of 1919 shows the impact of Kant's theory of philosophy on the early 19th century German Romantics. They had anticipated Benjamin in extending the Kantian problem of experience to include visual art. He presents two views of Romantic art criticism summed up by **A.W. von Schlegel** (1767-1845) and **J.W. von Goethe** (1749-1832).

THE MEANING OF THE WORK OF ART, FOR SCHLEGEL, IS INCOMPLETE AND IT IS THE TASK OF THE CRITIC TO COMPLETE IT AS FAR AS POSSIBLE

THE CRITIC HAS TO DRAW OUT AND INVENT NEW MEANINGS IN THE FACE OF THE WORK OF ART. WHEN THIS IS NO LONGER POSSIBLE, THE WORK OF ART HAS EXHAUSTED ITS INNER LIFE.

THE CONCEPT OF RUINATION

The view that Benjamin was to emphasize, both in his dissertation and subsequent work, was that of Schlegel.

Benjamin would later expand on this important theory of ruination.

The dissertation marked the end of Benjamin's academic success. His parents came to stay while he and Dora were in Iseltwald by Lake Brienz. He had tried to keep the news of his doctorate from them. Not out of modesty, but because he feared they would now expect him to get a job. His father was a typical businessman, and in financial crisis because of German inflation.

A good example of Benjamin's collectionism is the watercolour *Angelus Novus* by **Paul Klee** (1879-1940) that he purchased in Munich in the spring of 1921. He would meditate on this picture in his last work, "Thesis on the Philosophy of History", in 1940.

THE FAILED EDITOR

Benjamin conceived of his future as the editor of his own intellectual journal. His chance came in mid-1921 when he was offered the editorship of a journal by the cunning publisher Richard Weißbach.

The project was aborted by an insoluble conflict of interests.

Or to put it another way: there was a collision between highly antiquated notions of art patronage and commercial interests. It was to be the first of Benjamin's many "large scale defeats".

CONFLICT WITH THE GEORGE CIRCLE

The characterization of Goethe in Benjamin's 1919 doctoral dissertation was already distinct from the monumental image of the hero of German literature that developed after Goethe's death in 1832. This had been fostered by the vastly influential élite circle of aesthetes gathered around the German poet, **Stefan George** (1868-1933).

I RESPECT GEORGE'S WORK BUT FEEL EXTREMELY HOSTILE TO HIS DISCIPLES WHO DOMINATED THE PROFESSION OF LITERARY CRITICISM IN GERMANY FOR THE FIRST THREE DECADES OF THIS CENTURY.

GOETHE

Benjamin chose to attack the prevailing mythical image of Goethe propagated by George's disciple **Friedrich Gundolf** (1880-1931) in his 1916 biographical study.

He objected to Gundolf's hagiographical tendency to privilege the significance of autobiography in Goethe at the expense of Goethe's "modernity". Against this, Benjamin adopted an "immanent critique", meaning a close interpretation of a single text, Goethe's novel, *Elective Affinities* (1809). We shall see how the plot of this novel is echoed in Benjamin's own experience.

THE STORY OF *ELECTIVE AFFINITIES*

The aristocratic Eduard has married Charlotte. They live in a country estate and are joined by Eduard's gentleman friend the Captain, and then by Charlotte's niece, Ottilie. While Charlotte and the Captain struggle

against their growing attraction, first Eduard, and then finally the innocent Ottilie announce their love for each other. The fateful birth of a child by Eduard and Charlotte throws Ottilie into emotional turmoil which subsequently leads to two catastrophes.

First, there is the accidental drowning of the child in the lake. Second, Ottilie's guilt at her complicity in the situation causes her to renounce Eduard and seek shelter in a convent.

Ottilie chooses total passivity and refuses to speak or eat. She believes this will help her achieve not merely absolution but a form of holiness. Eduard soon follows her to the grave.

BENJAMIN'S AFFINITIES

Events in Benjamin's own life strangely mirror Goethe's story. Early in 1921, the marriage between Benjamin and Dora began to collapse. Benjamin's former schoolmate, **Ernst Schoen** (1894-1960), a musician, poet and translator, came to visit the Benjamin family.

DORA FELL MADLY IN LOVE WITH HIM.

FOLLOWING A PATTERN SIMILAR TO THE NOVEL'S PLOT, BENJAMIN FELL IN LOVE WITH ANOTHER VISITOR TO THE HOUSE, THE SCULPTRESS JULA COHN...

Yet, characteristically, Benjamin was unable to win Jula's love. It seems that women failed to find Benjamin sexually attractive.

THE TASK OF THE CRITIC

The title of Goethe's novel in German, *Die Wahlverwandtschaften*, comes from a technical term of 18th century chemistry. What it means in chemistry – as a fatally ironic symbol of the couples "cross-affined" in this story – is explained by the Captain in chapter four.

THOSE NATURES WHICH, WHEN THEY MEET, QUICKLY LAY HOLD ON AND MUTUALLY AFFECT ONE ANOTHER WE CALL AFFINED. THIS AFFINITY IS SUFFICIENTLY STRIKING IN THE CASE OF ALKALIS AND ACIDS WHICH, ALTHOUGH THEY ARE MUTUALLY ANTITHETICAL, AND PERHAPS PRECISELY BECAUSE THEY ARE SO, MOST DECIDEDLY SEEK AND EMBRACE ONE ANOTHER, MODIFY ONE ANOTHER, AND TOGETHER FORM A NEW SUBSTANCE...

THE AFFINITIES BECOME INTERESTING ONLY WHEN THEY BRING ABOUT DIVORCES.

The pun in German is *Scheidung* = divorce, *Scheidekünstler* = literally "divorce artist", but meaning analytical chemist. There is something of the *Scheidekünstler* in Benjamin.

Benjamin's truly magnificent essay, "Goethe's *Elective Affinities*", written in 1922, borrows its method of "immanent critique" from the German Romantics. It insists on a specific analysis of the novel in its own formal terms of myth and fate. But it is in fact coloured by events in Benjamin's own life. He consulted the sexologist **Charlotte Wolff** (1900-86) on his marital problems and crisis with Jula Cohn. What for? We might agree with the views of Wolff and Scholem.

GOETHE'S CHARACTERS ARE NOT AUTONOMOUS KANTIAN AGENTS MAKING CHOICES AND ENTERING INTO CONTRACTS, BUT ARE INVOLVED IN A DRAMA OF DESIRE AND DEATH BEYOND THEIR CONSCIOUS CONTROL.

BENJAMIN HAD ONLY REALLY COME TO DEVELOP HIS GREAT WORKS OF LITER~ATURE THROUGH HIS PERSONAL INVOLVEMENTS AND PROBLEMS.

I DIVULGE THE SIMPLE BUT HIDDEN TRUTH THAT THIS WORK AND ITS IN~SIGHTS WERE POSSIBLE ONLY BECAUSE THEY WERE WRITTEN BY BENJAMIN IN A HUMAN SITUATION THAT CORRESPONDED UN~CANNILY TO THAT OF THE NOVEL.

THE TASK OF THE TRANSLATOR

Benjamin's attack on the culturally dominant George circle continued with his translations of **Charles Baudelaire** (1821-67). Stefan George had himself produced a significant translation of Baudelaire's collection *Les Fleurs du Mal* which Benjamin criticized through his own translation.

His translation of Baudelaire's *Tableaux Parisiens* was prefaced by one of Benjamin's most read essays, "The Task of the Translator", written in 1921 and published in 1923. In it, Benjamin shifts the theoretical focus from the translation of individual words and phrases to the translation of one language into another. In translating Baudelaire into German, the German language is itself changed by the passage of the French poetry into it.

ALL GREAT TEXTS CONTAIN THEIR POTENTIAL TRANSLATION **BETWEEN THE LINES . . .**

Benjamin, always working "in the interests of language", was extending his theory of universal translation announced in the 1916 fragment, "On Language as Such and on the Language of Mankind".

THE BOOKMAN ...

Like most intellectuals, Benjamin had an ever-mushrooming library. And being constantly on the move, he constantly faced having to pack and unpack his books. In what was originally a radio broadcast, he reflected on the importance for him of book-collecting, where he had bought certain volumes, their value both sentimental and antiquarian, and on other people's reaction to the intellectual's fetishist delights of the library. This became the essay "Unpacking My Library" (1930).

One of the myths to be scotched is that Benjamin seldom published in his lifetime. In fact, besides three books, he published countless journal and newspaper articles, translated considerably, spoke at conferences and made over 90 radio broadcasts. As a cultural critic, Benjamin benefited from the Weimar Republic's booming media industries, and these, plus his commissions as a translator, provided his main sources of income in the 1920s and early 30s.

RIEGL VERSUS WÖLFFLIN

Benjamin's reputation as a literary critic and philosopher of language is secure. But his contribution to art criticism is greatly underestimated, thanks to the complexity and dispersal of his writings on art. The key to Benjamin's theory of art criticism is gained by understanding the opposed views of two major art historians, Heinrich Wölfflin and Alois Riegl. The first important difference between them is this.

WÖLFFLIN VIEWS ART HISTORY AS A SERIES OF STYLISTIC PHASES, JUDGED FORMALLY IN TERMS OF A **RISE** OR **FALL** IN ARTISTIC STANDARDS.

The Austrian art historian **Alois Riegl** (1858–1905) broke with this traditional formalism in his epochal work, *The Late Roman Art Industry* (1901). Until then, the art of Rome in its twilight years of domination in the West, around AD 400, had been judged in decline. Previous classical standards of artistic skill had collapsed. Riegl disagreed.

THE ART OF THE LATE ROMAN EMPIRE WAS NOT DECADENT BUT IN A NECESSARY STAGE OF TRANSITION FROM **ANCIENT** TO **MODERN**.

To explain this transition, Riegl introduced a concept that proved crucial to Benjamin: the *Kunstwollen*, a "will to art" or "an immanent artistic drive". This means there is always a fundamental *intention* which guides artistic production and ensures the continuity of art history.

63

THE TRANSITION FROM HAPTIC TO OPTIC

The impetus of the *Kunstwollen* can be represented by the transitions in antique art from *haptic* (tactile) to *optic* (space) elements. In the first basic or haptic phase, a close-sighted tactile view of objects emphasizes a clear outline against a ground, as in Egyptian art and hollow relief.

SUCH ART AVOIDS DETAILING ITS OBJECTS, FOR INSTANCE EITHER BY FORESHORTENINGS OR SHADOWS OR PARTICULAR FACIAL EXPRESSIONS.

A second phase continuing the haptic-optic levels of figuration is exemplified by classical Greek art, especially in its relief sculpture, which does contain elements of foreshortening and shadowing of the figures. But the optical or "spaced" viewpoint – in other words, the amount of *depth* – is still restricted.

THE FIGURES ARE FIRMLY LOCKED TO A TACTILE PLANE.

When we come to the third or optical phase, found in Late Roman art culture, objects stand in full three-dimension. The space between bodies appears measurable, and although still organized in relation to a plane, the objects have no tactile connection to it. This is achieved by deep shadowing and the objects tend to blur into their environment.

THE FIGURES ARE FIRMLY LOCKED TO A TACTILE PLANE.

This conception of "near"-versus-"far" spectatorial viewpoints will bear fruit in Benjamin's 1936 essay, "The Work of Art in the Age of Mechanical Reproduction".

As Benjamin put it, Riegl recognized a new experience of space and a new artistic volition (*Kunstwollen*) in what previously had been theorized as a "period of decline", "a regression into barbarism".

THE AESTHETICS OF DISINTEGRATION

Riegl himself, also like Benjamin, borrows from an "aesthetic of disintegration" in German Romantic art theory via Kant to **G.W.F. Hegel** (1770–1831). This aesthetic, in essence, values the breakdown of the natural tactile forms as a development in art which will lead the viewer to a "loss of self" in greater imaginative activity. Paradoxically, this disintegration of tactile coherence brings an increase of subjectivity and is a further step in the attainment of freedom.

In the group-portrait art of **Rembrandt** (1606–69), Riegl sees precisely this: a development of an optical *subjective* value.

Benjamin's own concept of **ruination** will extend the "aesthetics of disintegration" in his focus on the shift to modernity.

RIEGL'S STRUCTURALISM

There is another very important aspect to Riegl's method of art history. He does not accept the traditional hierarchy of "high", "minor" and "decorative" arts. They are all structurally interrelated. This permits him a structural investigation of the patterns of vegetal ornament from ancient Egyptian to Greek, Roman and Byzantine styles and their legacy in the "arabesque" of Islamic culture.

THE TASK OF THE ART CRITIC

Let's see how Riegl's example inspired Benjamin's own art criticism. A typical instance of this is found in "A Child's View of Colour", a fragment text of 1914–15.

Children are unconcerned with three-dimensionality which they perceive by touch, Benjamin says, which recalls Riegl's "haptic" first phase of art. Colour, in the pure image of the rainbow, represents the child's "life in art": and thereby the *Kunstwollen* is already identified in the child's world.

CHILDREN'S BOOKS

Colour is again central to Benjamin's interest in children's picture-books. He collected rare antique ones – and others for his son Stefan's use, but kept them safely out of his reach!

THE GAZING CHILD ENTERS INTO THESE PAGES, BECOMING SUFFUSED, LIKE A CLOUD, WITH THE RIOTOUS COLOURS OF THE WORLD OF PICTURES ...

Child-like openness and sophisticated erudition are Benjamin's hallmarks. His analysis of colour in children's art and picture-books feeds into reflections on the philosophy of art, as seen in two 1917 pieces, "Painting, or Signs and Marks" and "Painting and the Graphic Arts".

We can imagine Benjamin and Dora in 1917 visiting the Berlin art gallery *Der Sturm* and seeing modernist works by **Wassily Kandinsky** (1866–1944) and **Pablo Picasso** (1881–1973).

LINE OR COLOUR?

Benjamin's reflections on the "medium of the mark" carry on his debate with Wölfflin in Riegl's spirit.

Benjamin remains true to his philosophy of colour described in "The Rainbow" (1915). Colour does not have a fixed value and its values shift according to their relations with other colours.

Cubism's re-ordering of pictorial space made striking the poverty of Wölfflin's view. Cubist painting did not describe the figure through the application of line to a background, but rather, it fused figure and ground. Line emerged through the intersections of planes of colour.

THE OPTIC OF TECHNOLOGY

The lesson of modernist art for Benjamin was of a radical shift in **experience** itself. In the hierarchical model of tradition, experience is taken for granted as the ground on which (as Wölfflin might put it) the figure is delineated.

IN MODERN EXPERIENCE THERE IS NO LONGER AN ASSURED GROUND BUT A SHIFTING SET OF RELATIONS MADE POSSIBLE BY **TECHNOLOGY**

Benjamin had learned from Riegl that any hierarchy in the arts is unsustainable. Each art, including the popular media, represents an uncertain position within the technological organization of modern experience.

THE COLLECTOR

Passionate attention to the so-called minor genres of visual art is elegantly theorized in Benjamin's essay "Eduard Fuchs, Collector and Historian" (1937). He is sympathetic to Fuchs (1870–1940), an enlightened collector of Rabelaisian gusto, who wrote on the populist forms of caricature, erotic art and T'ang Dynasty ceramics.

In this essay, as elsewhere, Benjamin makes important observations on "high" art precisely through his attention to the previously considered "minor" art forms.

BENJAMIN THE NOMAD

Benjamin spent his life in nomadic quest for authentic modern experience. Travelling, "an international cultural action", was for him one of the definitive forms of that experience.

Benjamin's constant peregrinations gave him access to varieties of architecture, urbanism, art and political situations that coloured his experience of modernity.

Inflation and the atmosphere in Germany had become oppressive. In the spring of 1924 Benjamin went to Capri, an island in the bay of Naples, where he could live cheaply for six months. This was the first year of Mussolini's Fascist dictatorship in Italy. Here, as in post-war Germany, the attempt to organize a Soviet-style socialism, chiefly in Turin (1919-21), had ended in a crushing defeat and Fascism's triumph.

Benjamin habitually kept a diary when travelling. As early as 1913 he had written that the diary questions existence and "gives depth to time".

Benjamin frequented the Café Hidigeigei in Capri but mentions "hardly any noteworthy people here" among the German and other intellectuals he met. One notable exception was the maverick Marxist philosopher **Ernst Bloch** (1885–1977) who had impressed Benjamin at their first meeting in 1919 with the title of a book he was working on, *System of Theoretical Messianism*.

Benjamin later said of Bloch: "I revere him as the greatest connoisseur of my writings."

He mentions another café encounter with a Bolshevist Latvian woman from Riga, a theatre worker, Asja Lacis, which developed into a holiday romance.

Benjamin's own peculiar form of Marxism began to ripen with these café and bedroom discussions, but especially with his reading of *History and Class Consciousness* (1923) by **Georg Lukács** (1885–1971).

MEDIATION

A key concept in Lukács' work is **mediation**. It means there are no social "facts": no facet of social reality can be understood by any observer as final or complete in itself. Mediation recognizes that the particular "immediacy" of facts is constantly being overcome by "total" reality in the process of becoming. And the only form that proletarian consciousness must take to realize this surpassing of immediacy is in the Communist Party.

THE TOTAL CONSCIOUS WILL ITSELF OF THE PROLETARIAT CLASS **IS** THE COMMUNIST PARTY.

HE MAKES THE PROLETARIAT BOTH THE SUBJECT AND OBJECT OF HISTORY.

Lukács aimed to fulfil the classical German idealist goal of uniting freedom as an objective reality and as produced by humanity itself. It was an attempt, as Lukács himself later said, "to out-Hegel Hegel".

Reification is the major concern of Lukács: that which in the capitalist phase of history transforms social beings into *res*, "things" in Latin, and empties the world of sense. Everything is reified into *merchandise*, so that the world as a human production becomes hostile and strange. Hegel had named it "alienation", analyzed by Marx as "commodity fetishism". But what becomes of culture?

IS CULTURE ALSO ENTIRELY REIFIED?

THIS IS AN ERROR OF VULGAR MARXISTS. THEY REDUCE CULTURE TO A MERE 'REFLECTION' OF THE MATERIAL ECONOMIC BASE.

Lukács provided Benjamin with a sophisticated neo-Marxist theory of culture as a socially mediated force that could negate the status quo, not something explained away as "merely ideological".

THE BOLSHEVIK VERDICT

Lukács had been active as Commissar of Culture in yet another abortive Soviet Republic led by **Bela Kun** (1886–1939) in Hungary after the post-war collapse of the Austro-Hungarian Empire. It only lasted six months in 1919! His revolutionary credentials did not protect him from accusations of heresy by intellectuals of the Communist Third International.

Not only Communist but even Social-Democrat ideologues in Weimar attacked the book. Lukács himself was forced to repudiate it.

Lukács' early "idealist" work influenced the Frankfurt School of neo-Marxism and later the New Left. But it is telling that Benjamin should be attracted to ideas that fell outside orthodox Marxism. Lukács took the pessimistic view that consciousness in modern capitalist society was inescapably determined by the conditions of the market.

Benjamin's essay "Naples" (1925), written with Asja Lacis, introduces the central concept of **porosity** understood in both spatial and temporal terms.

SPATIAL AND TEMPORAL POROSITY

Naples is spatially porous in its mingling of private and public: the home spills out into the street. Similarly, it has no temporal fixity.

"What distinguishes Naples from other large cities is something it has in common with the African Kraal; each private attitude or act is permeated by streams of communal life. Here there is interpenetration of day and night, street and home."

Although celebrating the porosity of Naples, he also saw another side to it. The opportunities for improvization and unexpected movement around the city also provided the conditions for the organized crime of the Mafia-style *camorra*. Benjamin saw three intersecting networks of power in Naples.

A DICTATOR'S VISIT

One specific event stands out from Benjamin's recollections of Naples – the visit of the Fascist dictator **Benito Mussolini** (1883–1945). "All kinds of festive decorations failed to deceive anyone about the coldness with which the people received the event."

Benjamin here anticipates Hitler's march through Berlin in 1933 after assuming power, an event of far more dreadful significance for the future of modernity.

INTRODUCING THE ARCADE

One example of porosity given in the "Naples" essay was the arcade, its first appearance in Benjamin's writing. "In a glass-roofed bazaar there is a toyshop that would hold its own beside fairy-tale galleries." There was a vogue for building arcades in the early to mid-19th century which exploited the new possibilities of iron and glass technology.

The arcade Victor Emmanuel in Naples was one of the grandest ever built.

Benjamin saw in the arcade the architectural prototype of the department store.

Benjamin's interest in the philosophy of glass came from the science-fiction writer **Paul Scheerbart**'s *Glass Architecture* (1914). This new form revolutionized modern life precisely by breaking down the distinctions between private and public – the very thing that had so enthralled Benjamin in the streets of Naples.

The antithesis of Neapolitan "porosity" was Benjamin's experience of Berlin with its clear, policed boundaries between private and public, street and home. **Dan Graham** (b. 1942), the Jewish-American Conceptual artist, also noticed this phenomenon in his home city of New York. Yet, in New York, this condition was the result of the modernist International Style of glass architecture which, contrary to its initial ideal of transparency, in fact mirrors the surroundings and thus enforces the demarcation between private and public realms.

In 1978, Graham designed a house of "porosity" – *Alteration to a Suburban House* – as a critique of boundary-policing evident in most cities.

PAST, PRESENT AND FUTURE

We have leapt ahead to an example of postmodern Conceptual art so as to emphasize the direction of Benjamin's thinking on modernism in 1924. His encounter with "outsider" Marxism at the time served only to confirm and intensify his project to trace the origins of modern experience. This project required him to map the past, present and future of modern and specifically capitalist forms of experience.

Benjamin would focus on the tensions, the possibilities and the betrayals of the political and technological revolutions in the 19th and 20th centuries.

Benjamin paid Moscow a visit from 6 December 1926 to 1 February 1927. He wished to experience at first hand Russia's "socialist exit" from capitalist modernity. He arrived at a critical turning-point in the Soviet Union. **Lenin** (1870–1924) had introduced his New Economic Policy (NEP) in 1921, a temporary "coexistence" of Communism and capitalism, or "State Capitalism", which partly liberalized the market. What Benjamin observed was state corruption with privileged Party officials, the instant millionaire "Nepmen" and mass poverty in the streets.

This was on the eve of **Stalin**'s (1879–1953) ruthless dictatorship and the imposition of his first Five Year Plan which would bring mass exterminations and the Gulag system.

Benjamin's other personal motive was to visit his "holiday lover", Asja Lacis, in a mental asylum following a breakdown. His portrait of Moscow is indeed of a madhouse, a tense atmosphere of suspicion and fear. Police state rule had instilled a Kafkaesque mentality in the people. No one dared voice an opinion but instead tried to guess what the next twist in the Party line might be.

Benjamin witnessed the post-mortem cult of Lenin with its iconic images and figures of every size, pose and material, omnipresent from public institutions to kitchens and laundries.

Benjamin foresaw a possible fusion emerging between the state and organized crime, not in the chaotic sense of Naples' *camorra*, but in the efficient Stalinist secret police. He had theoretically anticipated that possibility in his "Critique of Violence" (1921) which described police power as "formless, a nowhere-tangible, all-pervasive ghostly presence".

Benjamin donated the money for a goose to be shared at Christmas dinner with Asja. It was badly cooked and divided between six to eight other people sitting round a desk. Only Russian was spoken and Asja tired of translating for him.

There was no hope for Benjamin in the Soviet Union. Moscow represented an urban future that he found extremely unattractive. And although he had separated from Dora in 1923 (finally divorced in 1930), his relationship with Asja was over.

Benjamin left Moscow with at least two positive lessons. One, through Asja's guidance, was the stimulation of the Russian theatre which would open his eyes to the avant-garde work of the German Marxist playwright **Bertolt Brecht** (1898–1956). The other was a renewed conviction that he needed to deepen his understanding of the origins of capitalism.

SOVEREIGN VIOLENCE

Let's go back to 1921 when Benjamin began elaborating a political philosophy, inspired by a number of heterodox sources, chief among them Ernst Bloch's work of Expressionist philosophy *The Spirit of Utopia* (1918) and George Sorel's anarchistic *Reflections on Violence* (1908). "The Critique of Violence", the main surviving fragment of Benjamin's projected book on political philosophy, takes an anarchistic position on the modern liberal state.

THE MODERN STATE IS BASED ON THE LAW PRESERVING VIOLENCE, INCARNATED IN PRIVATE PROPERTY AND PROTECTED BY THE SPECTRAL VIOLENCE OF THE POLICE.

Benjamin contrasts the instrumental violence of the liberal police state with the "sovereign violence" of the "proletarian general strike".

In regarding the general strike as a form of "divine violence", Benjamin contributed to a current of early 1920s political theology, exemplified by **Carl Schmitt**'s contemporary *Political Theology* (1934). Schmitt, an arch-conservative opponent of liberal democracy, became a Nazi in the 1930s.

THE RELIGION OF CAPITALISM

This relationship between Benjamin's political thought and his aesthetic and philosophical concerns found expression in a fascinating correspondence with the Protestant conservative Florens Christian Rang (whose death in 1923 deeply affected him). How typical of Benjamin this is, to benefit from diverse and apparently incompatible sources!

Benjamin's interest in the Reformation, evident in the 1921 fragment, "Capitalism as Religion", anticipates some arguments later developed in his major works, *The Origin of German Tragic Drama* and the *Arcades Project*.

The debate on the origins of capitalist modernity had been initiated by the German sociologist **Max Weber** (1864–1920) who argued in his influential *The Protestant Ethic and the Spirit of Capitalism* (1904) that Protestantism was crucial in the formation of capitalism. In "Capitalism as Religion", Benjamin criticized Weber for not being radical enough.

THE EARLY PROTESTANTS INTERPRETED ECONOMIC SUCCESS AS A SIGN OF BEING AMONG THE HEAVENLY ELECT.

NO, IT'S NOT THAT THE PROTESTANT FAITH ENCOURAGED CAPITALISM, BUT THAT CAPITALISM ITSELF BECAME A RELIGION

Capitalism was a parasite of Reformation Christianity that took over its host.

What we have, in Benjamin's words, is capitalism's "expulsion of despair", a curious state in which despair itself becomes a religious condition of the world in the hope that this will lead to salvation. "God's transcendence is at an end."

THE ORIGIN OF GERMAN TRAGIC DRAMA

This is a study of Reformation culture in the stage of capitalist transition. Literally the "stage", since Benjamin's model is the Baroque form of the *Trauerspiel* or mourning-play. The book's dedication "Conceived 1916 – Written 1925" stresses the continuity between it and the 1916 fragments on the differences between classical tragedy and the mourning-play (see pages 33-37). The key to the mourning-play is to ask – what is being *mourned*? And why with such ostentation? Or as the playwright **Daniel Caspers von Lohenstein** (1635–83) puts it ...

A play wherein one man now enters and another exits;
With tears it begins and with weeping ends.
Yea, after death itself, time with us still toys,
When foul maggot and worm drill our putrid corpses ...

These are plays for the *satisfaction of the mournful* which require Baroque excess.

WHAT IS "BAROQUE"?

The origin of the term *baroque* is uncertain. Some argue that it comes from "rough-shaped pearl"; others that it refers to "absurd", "bizarre" or "extravagant". Baroque differs slightly in its application to art and architecture, literature and music. This allegorical painting by **Jacopo Tintoretto** (1518–94), "The Origin of the Milky Way", displays baroque features of "bizarre extravagance".

The Baroque speaks in allegory.

This allegorical image of "milkiness" pairs nicely with another by the Baroque poet, **Richard Crashaw** (1612?–49), an English convert to Catholicism at the height of the Counter-Reformation. One stanza from his poem on St Mary Magdalene suffices to illustrate the bizarre spinning out of a "mournful" metaphor.

Lo where a Wounded Heart *with Bleeding* Eyes *conspire.*
Is she a Flaming *Fountain, or a* Weeping *fire!*

Upwards thou dost weep.
Heav'n's bosom drinks the gentle stream.
Where th'milky rivers creep,
Thine floats above; and is the cream.
Waters above th' Heav'ns, what they be
We' are taught best by thy *Tears* and thee.

But what was *in* the Baroque climate that encouraged such extravagant allegory?

105

POLITICAL THEOLOGIES

The essential doctrine of the Protestant Reformation laid down by **Martin Luther** (1483–1546) was that salvation depended on grace through *faith alone*, which denied any spiritual effect to human action. Life was devalued by faith and *melancholy* was the inevitable outcome. The mourning-play gives us the world revealed in the gaze of isolated melancholy man.

Instead, the Catholic reaction to Protestantism in the Counter-Reformation reasserted the *redemptive* authority of the Church, gave power to the Jesuits and extended the Inquisition, but also revived Catholic spirituality in the secular realm.

Lohenstein, **Andreas Gryphius** (1616–64) and other German writers of the Baroque *Trauerspiel* were all Lutherans. Benjamin makes the point that Shakespeare and the Catholic Spaniard **Calderón de la Barca** (1600–81) created far more important mourning-plays than these largely forgotten German ones. There are nevertheless certain formal elements of the genre which they all share – beginning with the "world as the stage", "a setting for mournful events".

A NIHILISTIC TOY-BOX

If the stage is a coffin, it is also the world's toy-box from which pantomime players emerge, typified by their roles: the evil intriguing courtier (Iago); the absent or dreamer hero (Hamlet); the king, hybrid of tyrant and martyr, either usurping or usurped (Hamlet's father); the parody commentators, clowns, fools and jesters.

The ensemble reminds one of playing-card figures — but the game is pointless

Actions in the mourning-play do not add up. Speech and gesture mislead, decisions are postponed, and the end is nihilistic catastrophe: such as Hamlet's "accidental" death by a poisoned rapier.

THERE IS A SPECIAL PROVIDENCE IN THE FALL OF A SPARROW...

These playing-card figures appear to enact the Baroque circumstances of closed theologies, of emerging Divine Right monarchs and absolutist states, but in fact they mourn the off-stage transition to capitalist modernity. The world is drained of meaning and the only bleak Lutheran hope is that absurd meaninglessness can become the source of salvation.

SYMBOL, ALLEGORY AND RUINATION

Benjamin opens his study with a daunting "Epistemo-Critical Prologue" in which he tackles the problem of *origin*. Origin is described as "an eddy in the stream of becoming", in other words, something that is both *in* and *out* of time. This peculiarity of origin – outside time but open to its effects – permits him to identify **allegory** as the key feature of Baroque culture.

CLASSICAL TRAGEDY HINGES ON THE **SYMBOL** WHICH PRESENTS A TIMELESS TRUTH IN THE BEAUTIFUL APPEARANCE, EVEN IF IMPERFECTLY.

ALLEGORY INSTEAD PRESENTS THE **TEMPORARINESS** OF TRUTH IN THE RUINATION OF APPEARANCE.

This is summed up in Benjamin's famous aphorism.

"Allegories are in the realm of thoughts what ruins are in the realm of things."

The mourning-play was conceived from the outset as a **ruin**. Now it becomes clear that Benjamin's analysis of allegory in Baroque drama revealed to him the origin of modernity. The fragmented nature of modern experience – the way it is experienced discontinuously as shock – was "originally" manifested through Baroque allegories of ruination and *transience*.

"All that is solid melts into air, all that is holy is profaned, and man is at last compelled to face with sober senses, his real conditions of life ..." Karl Marx, *Manifesto of the Communist Party*, 1848

A UNIVERSITY SCANDAL

In 1925, Benjamin made one last desperate effort to gain the *Habilitation* (qualification for a university teaching post) and secure his financial independence. He submitted his *Trauerspiel* study as a qualifying thesis to Franz Schulz, professor of literary history at the University of Frankfurt. This proved another of Benjamin's "large scale defeats".

And so, the *Trauerspiel* went round the various departments on a voyage of scandalous incomprehension, until Benjamin withdrew it. "Better to be chased off in disgrace than retreat."

It was as if Benjamin had fallen victim to the intriguing courtiers in a Baroque academic pantomime. Once again, his *Angelus Novus* was grounded, indeed, stripped of its beauty.

Benjamin published *The Origin of German Tragic Drama* with Rowohlt in 1928.

A FAIRYTALE FOR ACADEMICS

Today, we still find a fragmented Benjamin circulating the university departments, in a different sense now, as each one tries to claim "their" piece of him. Benjamin perhaps foresaw this in a sly allegorical fairytale he wrote that was originally intended to preface *The Origin of German Tragic Drama*, but was dropped.

I would like to tell the story of Sleeping Beauty a second time

She sleeps in her hedge of thorns. And after so many years, she awakens

But not from the kiss of a Prince Charming. The cook it was who awoke her, when he gave the skullery boy a resounding slap that echoed throughout the castle with the pent-up force of so many years.

A beautiful child lies sleeping behind the thorny hedge of the following pages.

Let no Prince Charming clad in the shining armour of modern scholarship venture too close. For as he embraces his bride she will bite him.

To awaken her, the author has, instead, reserved for himself the role of the cook. Too long has the slap been overdue that is intended to send reverberations through the corridors of academic scholarship.

The academic *débâcle* may have hastened Benjamin's involvement with Marxism. He turned to writing for a wider media-receptive public, exemplified by *One-Way Street*, also published in 1928. This short work, of fragmentary observations and lists, combines allegory with the style of the New Objectivity (*Neue Sachlichkeit*), a dominant art movement in late 1920s' Germany. The new style reflected the increasing coldness of modern urban experience: a clinical refusal of emotion, a cynical presentation of the world "as it is", and a cult of technology.

Bus conductors, officials, workmen, salesmen – they all demonstrate the menace of the material world through their own surliness.

SCENES FROM ONE-WAY STREET: WRITING

Benjamin foresees a "picture-writing of the future" in graphic stages.

1. writing begins gradually to lie down ...

from upright inscriptions, to manuscripts on sloping desks and finally to bed in the printed book ...

2. writing begins to rise up again …

newspapers are read in the vertical, film and advertisements dictate the perpendicular …

3. the book is outdated by the three-dimensionality of the card-index filing system …

4. a leap into future graphic regions: statistical and technical diagrams – an international *moving script* – and into the "ether" of the Internet …

... AND TECHNOLOGY

Benjamin meditates in allegorical "new objective" style on the potential gains and perils of modern technology.

The dark night of war-time annihilation shook us like the aura of bliss that the epileptic experiences in seizure. The revolutions after it were mankind's first attempts to bring this new body under control.

BENJAMIN, THE SURREALIST

Benjamin's writing has much in common with Surrealism's "irruption of the Unconscious" in everyday life, a link not sufficiently appreciated. His essay, "Surrealism: the Last Snapshot of the European Intelligentsia" (1929), defines *profane illumination* as Surrealism's true revolutionary aim, something that can begin with hashish or opium, but which is less dangerously effective than the "narcotic of thinking". This could well describe Benjamin himself. And it is again with himself in mind that he names "the project around which Surrealism circles in all its books and enterprises". What is this project?

He scolds the Surrealists for their flirtations with the occult and spiritualism, but this could also be a self-criticism of the mysticism in his own nature. In fact, many Surrealists became Communists in the 1920s.

TEDDY AND BERT

Benjamin's friendships, like his life, seem dictated by coincidences, good and bad. He could have lamented, in Aristotle's words, "O my friends, there is no friend." Gershom Scholem, settled in Palestine in 1923, continued to advise and scold him as a "voice afar" from the sunny Promised Land. Two other friendships grew complex but also very productive in the 1930s: with Theodor ("Teddy") Wiesengrund Adorno and Bertolt ("Bert") Brecht, the polar opposites of contemporary Marxism.

THE FRANKFURT INSTITUTE

T.W. Adorno (1903-69) was one of the luminaries of the Frankfurt Institute of Social Research, founded in 1923, an influential assembly of social scientists, philosophers and psychoanalysts, aiming to update Marxism and radically dissect modern society. The Institute coined the now freely-used term, "Critical Theory", as an antidote to the non-critical fashions of phenomenology, logical positivism and dogmatic Stalinist Marxism. Their non-dogmatic theory of "dialectical materialism" and astonishing range of interests in aesthetics, film, mass culture and politics were congenial to Benjamin.

WE HAVE TO CONFRONT THE MODERN CONDITIONS OF CAPITALISM WHICH HAVE DEVELOPED SINCE MARX'S DAY

THEY SHARE MY FRAGMENTARY APPROACH TO MODERNITY... BESIDES, THE INSTITUTE CAN ASSIST ME

True, the Institute published Benjamin and financially assisted him. But the irony is that **Max Horkheimer** (1895-1973), director of the Institute from 1930 onwards, had been among those Frankfurt University academics who had denied Benjamin the *Habilitation* thesis in 1925.

DISSIMILAR SIMILARITIES

While the Marxist radicalism of Adorno and his colleagues would seem to presuppose revolution, in reality, as Martin Jay, the historian of the Institute, observed, "… the Frankfurt School chose the purity of its theory over affiliation" to any party, SDP, Communist or any other. Indeed, this was a "school" of Marxism best adapted to conditions which did not yet prevail – the Cold War and the "New Left" currents of the 1950s and 60s. Such "purity" was reflected in Adorno's elegant, densely-muscled prose style – the polar extreme to Brecht's simple economy of expression.

"Crude thinking", characterized by Macheath in Brecht's best-known work, *The Threepenny Opera* (1928), means simplifying thought to crystallize it for revolutionary **practice**.

Benjamin had first met "Teddy" at Frankfurt University in 1923; but their association matured in the 1930s. He also frequented Brecht (1898-1956) in the 30s: they were introduced by Asja Lacis in 1929. Brecht often mercilessly chastized Benjamin, calling him *Würstchen* (little sausage). Scholem remarked that Benjamin was drawn to Brecht's harsh "athletic" qualities. But there was empathy and a deep similarity, despite their differences.

Let's see what is meant by the Brechtian strategies of *Ermattungstaktik* (tactics of attrition) and *Jetztzeit* (the presence of the now).

"THE HARD THING GIVES WAY"

The "tactic of attrition" is summed up in Brecht's poem on the Chinese sage Lao Tzu whose maxim is "The hard thing gives way."

A "promise and a lesson" of what? Formed by the victories of Fascism and the degeneration of socialism in the USSR, Brecht and Benjamin share a materialist pessimism which is really designed for **hope**: for a longer-term survival in what they foresee as another Dark Age millennium. Survival needs cunning, "water-like" pliancy and anonymity – the virtues of **attrition**.

"THE PRESENCE OF THE PAST, NOW"

"Only the historian will have the gift of fanning the spark of hope in the past who is firmly convinced that even the dead will not be safe from the enemy if he wins." This is from Benjamin's "Sixth Thesis on the Philosophy of History" (1940) which expresses his constant vigilance to reclaim the past on behalf of its victims. But how can this square with Brecht's insistence on the *Jetztzeit*, "the presence of the now"?

The revolutionary presence of the **now** "blasts open the continuum of history". In this sense, time is redeemed; and in this sense only does the Messiah arrive.

THE ART OF MONTAGE

Tactical "crude thinking" in the sly Brechtian manner was necessarily allied to **allegorical** thinking as Benjamin developed it. As writers, both were also natural magpies alert to the fragmentation of modern experience. The instinct to scavenge the significant fragment and connect dis-similarities in order to shock an audience into fresh recognition – this was the essence of Brecht's aesthetic.

AND ITS NAME IS THE ART OF **MONTAGE**

ALLEGORY REFLECTED THE **MELANCHOLY** ORIGIN OF CAPITALISM. MONTAGE IS THE **UN**-MELANCHOLY FORM OF MODERN TECHNOLOGY.

Brecht had mastered the lesson of montage in the popular media of newspapers, radio and film. Into this form ("the bad new things"), he poured the content of revolutionary Marxism.

From the island of Ibiza (on the move again!), Benjamin contemplated the inauguration of the Third Reich in January 1933.

Benjamin was already considering exile. He was in no doubt (and with chilling foresight) that Nazi Germany was "a train that does not leave until everyone is on board".

THE GREAT DICTATOR ...

Benjamin did return to Berlin and witnessed the early months of book burnings, violent street scenes and Hitler's hysterical speeches.

THE AIR IS NOT FIT TO BREATHE ANYMORE, NOT THAT THIS MATTERS IF ONE IS BEING STRANGLED ANYWAY. ABOVE ALL ECONOMICALLY.

His own economic situation was deteriorating badly. Newspaper editors would not allow him to publish, except under a pseudonym. In the middle of March, he left for Paris. "Where else but Paris?"

Benjamin often visited Brecht in his own exile at Svendborg, Denmark. They heard Hitler's 1934 Reichstag Speech on the radio and compared the "great dictator" to the film star "little tramp", Charlie Chaplin.

THE FASHIONABLE IDEAL SET BY HITLER IS NOT THAT OF THE ARMY BUT RATHER OF THE "DISTINGUISHED GENTLEMEN". SO MUCH GLITTER SURROUNDING SO MUCH SHABBINESS.

HM! BUT YOU ALSO HAVE TO IMAGINE CHAPLIN AS A MAFIOSO GANG LEADER.

IT IS OF NO SERVICE IN UNDER-STANDING HITLER TO REPRESENT HIM AS A CARTOON GANGSTER.

Brecht's play, *The Resistible Rise of Arturo Ui* (1941), depicted Hitler as a small-time racketeer who makes it big by "massaging his image". This was scathingly criticized by Adorno.

THE AUTHOR AS PRODUCER

In Paris, 24 April 1934, at the Institute for the Study of Fascism, Benjamin gave his notorious reading of "The Author as Producer". He called on the artists on the left "to side with the proletariat". In Paris at the time, this call was not radical; the approach, however, was. In true Brechtian style, Benjamin urged the "advanced" artist to intervene, like the revolutionary worker, in the means of artistic production – to change the "technique" of traditional media.

TRANSFORM THE APPARATUS OF BOURGEOIS CULTURE. DO NOT ADOPT THE AESTHETICALLY CONSERVATIVE POSITION OF PRESENTING A REVOLUTIONARY CONTENT BY MEANS OF TRADITIONAL FORMS.

As a model of "radical form and content", Benjamin offered the newspaper: "a vast melting-down process which not only destroys the conventional separation between genres, between writer and poet, scholar and popularizer, but also questions even the separation between author and reader."

THE PLACE WHERE THE WORD IS MOST DEBASED — THE NEWSPAPER — BECOMES THE VERY PLACE WHERE A RESCUE OPERATION IS MOUNTED.

Benjamin had apparently digested Brecht's crude-thinking formula of "bad new things" and the hope placed in revolution by attrition. Despite this, Brecht would always claim that he never knew what Benjamin was on about!

THE AGE OF REPRODUCTION

Benjamin's 1936 essay, "The Work of Art in the Age of Mechanical Reproduction", is perhaps his best-known but often misunderstood work. Let's begin by sampling Benjamin's analysis of cinema as a technical reorganization of reality.

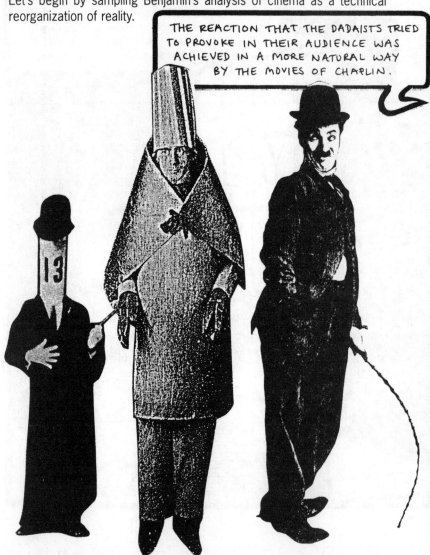

"The film is the art form that is in keeping with the increased threat to his life that modern man has to face." That "threat" was evidenced by the overture of the Spanish Civil War (1936-39).

THE PAINTER AND THE CAMERA-MAN

The first Blitzkrieg bombing of an urban population befell the Basque capital of **Guernica** (1937), "immortalized" by Picasso's painting of that event. We might ask, in Benjamin's spirit, how does the painter compare with the camera-man in such an age of mass destruction? The painter is like the magician who heals the sick by the "laying on of hands".

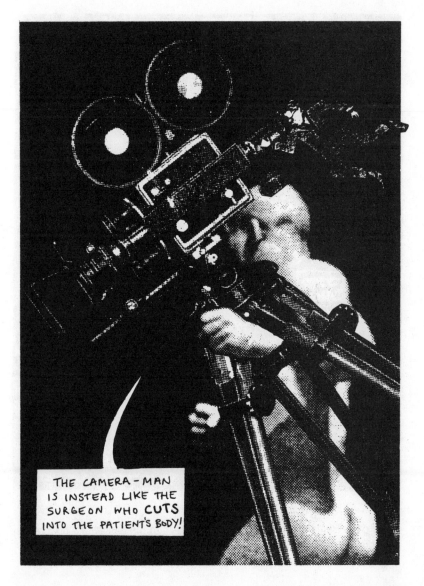

THE CAMERA-MAN IS INSTEAD LIKE THE SURGEON WHO CUTS INTO THE PATIENT'S BODY!

MASS REPRODUCTION

Benjamin was deeply concerned with the consequent impact on art of the mass technologies of reproduction. What happens to an "immortal" painting – say, Van Gogh's *Sunflowers* – when it is mechanically reproduced on postcards, posters or even postage stamps **without regard** to its original size, location or history?

What does Benjamin mean by "aura"? It refers to the customary historical role played by works of art – their "ritual function" – in the legitimation of traditional social formations.

Throughout the history of culture, works of art depended on a **status**: they owed their existence primarily to their implication in the processes of social integration. As an object of religious veneration and worship, the work of art acquires a "halo" of *uniqueness* and *authenticity*. And so, Benjamin arrives at his famous definition of the aura …

THE UNIQUE PHENOMENON OF DISTANCE, HOWEVER CLOSE AN OBJECT MAY BE.

Auratic "distance" is in this sense *unmeasurable*. We should also note that Benjamin's terminology here is still guided by Riegl – and so too is the brief history of art he develops.

Renaissance painting, with its cult of secular beauty, first challenged the ritualistic basis of artistic production. A long, hard struggle for artistic autonomy then began, which, via Romanticism, culminated in the pinnacle of **aestheticism** …

... THE DECADENT "ART FOR ART'S SAKE" EPISODE AT THE END OF THE 19th CENTURY.

This last decadent attempt to restore the "venerable" aura within the ghetto of aestheticism occurred as a reaction against the rampant commodification of art under 19th century capitalism. But the emergence of "Art for Art's Sake" coincides with photography and the crisis of painting.

THE DECAY OF THE AURA

The increasing intervention of technology in the production and reception of works of art tends to dissolve them and, in the 20th century, results in the decay of the aura. To substitute a plurality of mechanically reproduced copies for the unique original must destroy the very basis for the production of auratic works of art – that singularity in time and space on which they depend for their claim to authority and authenticity.

UNCERTAINTIES AND AMBIGUITIES

Although "transformation by technology" might contain radical potentials for the political deployment of art, Benjamin was in fact equivocal, because he could see how it could also be co-opted to support traditional or even reactionary and Fascist politics. Indeed, his adoption of Brechtian "crude" tactics becomes fully intelligible in the glare of Fascism's own crass but powerful aestheticization of political violence. Benjamin's counterposal was to meet force with force. "Mankind which in Homer's time was an object of contemplation for the Olympic gods, now is one for itself ..."

Hence, his famous proclamation: "This is the situation in politics which Fascism is rendering aesthetic. Communism responds by politicizing art."

The loss of "auratic distance" might signal the era of a new ethical order based on the universal equality of things and the sovereignty of individuals. In short, the end of fetishized commodities and alienated consumers. But his ambiguity about this loss is shown in an earlier essay, "A Short History of Photography" (1931). Here he praises Atget who always photographed Paris without people, as a surreal *empty location*.

THEY ARE LIKE THE SCENES OF CRIMES THAT HARBOUR SOME GUILTY SECRET

He proclaims the photographer's task as "to uncover guilt in his pictures". What guilt? There is no evidence of any crime in Atget's pictures: they are empty. It is not so much that Atget liberates the object from the aura, but that the power of his photographs resides in their *suggested possession* of an aura.

CRITICISMS OF BENJAMIN'S POSITION

Benjamin has been shown to be mistaken. Mass reproduction actually *increases* aura – in an unforeseen way. Think of Van Gogh's *Sunflowers* again. Its mass-reproduced availability has in fact multiplied the aura of its *cash-value* and re-distanced it to the remote region of the uniquely priceless.

But in 1936, for different reasons, the essay troubled Max Horkheimer (now exiled with other Institute members in New York) and Adorno.

Beyond the time-bound circumstances of politics and polemics, Benjamin's "mistakes" remain creative, precisely because of the unresolved ambiguities of the "aura" that have yet to be explored.

Adorno, then in England until his move to New York in 1938, would often see his friend in Paris. He criticized Benjamin's essay for its "undialectical" acceptance of mechanically reproduced art and its rejection of all autonomous art as being inherently "counter-revolutionary". It failed to consider that some modernist art had radically divested itself of the retrograde aura in favour of a fragmentary and dissonant formal aesthetic structure – for instance, the twelve-tone music of **Arnold Schoenberg** (1874–1951).

KAFKA AND BENJAMIN'S MYSTICISM

In fact, Benjamin had already written an essay, "Franz Kafka", in 1934. He chose to write this commemorative piece on the 10th anniversary of Kafka's death (1883-1924) under the thatched roof of Brecht's cottage in Svendborg where he suffered Bert's acerbic criticisms.

Kafka's images are good, but the rest is pure mystification. It's nonsense. You have to ignore it. Depth doesn't get you anywhere at all...

The conversation then broke off to listen to the news from Vienna.

Benjamin's intense engagement with Kafka's work began with a short esoteric text, "Idea for a Mystery Play" (1927). He reviewed Kafka's story, "The Great Wall of China", for the radio in 1931. But why discuss Kafka with an unsympathetic Brecht? Scholem has wisely commented on this: "In those reflections on Kafka, his 'Janus face', as Benjamin liked to call it, assumed sharp contours. One side of it was offered to Brecht, the other to me."

143

THE KABBALA

Scholem had introduced Benjamin to the Kabbala, an esoteric system of Jewish Gnosticism, and its classic text, the 13th century *Zohar*, written in Spain. Scholem had also advised him to begin his inquiry on Kafka with the Book of Job: "… or at least with the possibility of divine judgement, which I regard as the sole subject of Kafka's production. Here, for once, a world is expressed in which redemption cannot be anticipated. Go and explain this to the *goyim!*" *Goyim*, i.e., the Gentiles – meaning presumably Brecht?

QABBALA

Kafka's outlook is that of a man caught under the wheels!

QUELLEN UND FORSCHUNGEN

ZUR GESCHICHTE DER

JÜDISCHEN MYSTIK

WHICH BENJAMIN?

Strange, that Benjamin's essay, steeped in years of Jewish mysticism, should coincide in 1934 with "The Author as Producer". So, which is the "real" Benjamin – the Marxist? the Jewish mystic? We should not see Benjamin's plural areas of work in contradiction or opposition to each other, but rather in continuous dialogue with each other. Intellectual, spiritual and political commitments need not be forced into a straitjacket, as Benjamin himself stated.

MY STANCE IS TO BEHAVE ALWAYS RADICALLY, NEVER CONSISTENTLY WHEN IT COMES TO THE MOST IMPORTANT THINGS.

As the *Zohar* says: "... then will the worlds be in harmony and all will be united into one, but until the future world is set up, this light is put away and hidden."

ORIGINS OF THE ARCADES PROJECT

Paris was Benjamin's "chosen city", as Martin Jay writes, "both as the site of his exile and as the controlling metaphor of his work". This is early evident in his passion for the "allegorist" poet of Paris, Charles Baudelaire. But the idea for an article on the Paris arcades began on a walk with his friend Franz Hessel, then, in 1926, collaborating with Benjamin on the translation of Marcel Proust's *À la recherche du temps perdu*.

A CENTRAL ARCHITECTURAL MOTIF

The first Paris arcades, constructed early in the 19th century, sometimes enclosed a number of streets under a glass roof. What attracted Benjamin was the simultaneity of being both outside and inside, the Neapolitan experience of "porosity" again, but especially the fashionable rows of shops with their dazzling displays of commodities behind glass façades.

HERE IS THE "OPEN SESAME" ENTRANCE TO PENET~ RATING THE MYSTERY OF COMMODITY FETISHISM...

Notes, plans and drafts began to accumulate between 1927 and 1929 for an essay with the indicative title of "Paris Arcades: A Dialectical Fairytale".

A MARATHON PROJECT

Discussions in 1929 at the resort of Bad Königstein with Adorno, Horkheimer and Asja Lacis gave the arcades project clearer Marxist shape. In Benjamin's mind, it had close allegorical links with his *Trauerspiel* thesis as a further epistemological "tragic drama" of the 19th century. Some five years later, in his Paris exile, research had got out of hand as Benjamin burrowed like a mole deep into the archives of the Bibliothèque Nationale.

Benjamin had not foreseen that his project would inflate into a massively *unfinishable* task – a stage of grim battles with the New York Institute over publication, and a race against the clock as war threatened.

MATERIALIST VENTRILOQUISM

Unfinishable or not, what was Benjamin's aim? It was to treat the bygone relics of the arcades period – its architecture, technologies and artefacts – with "utmost concreteness" as the precursors of modernity, in other words, as the *past witnesses of the present*. This was not merely "industrial archaeology" but an allegorical prompting of these dead witnesses to speak again of their "secret affinities" to our own time.

THE MAVERICK HISTORIAN

Ideology is whatever we take for granted as the God-given, natural or inevitable "facts" of economic, social and political life. Marx had performed a first deconstruction of the ideological assumptions underpinning the capitalist economy. The problem was that Marxism's faith in the march of historical progress had blinded it to other compulsions that might account for historical *regressions*. Fascism, in Benjamin's maverick view, was just such a phenomenon. It was not a sudden regression to barbarism but a return of compulsions already prepared deep within the "advanced culture" of 19th century capitalism. Freudians might call it "the return of the repressed". Another problem was that Marxist ideological criticism offered *theories* about social experience, not the experience itself.

PHANTASMAGORIA AND DIALECTICAL IMAGES

Phantasmagoria, a term used in Marx's *Das Kapital*, were optical devices for rapidly shifting the size of objects on a screen. Here was Benjamin's clue to depicting sensual immediacy. Capitalist modernity had come to focus in Paris under the monarchy of **Louis Philippe** (1830–48) and the Second Empire of **Napoleon III** (1852–70). How could he show the *regressive elements* and *utopian potentials* of this culture in graspable, powerful "dialectical images"? He began systematizing his mountain of research notes into colour-coded index cards.

Another guide to this vast unending maze of materials was a "blueprint" outline that he provided for Adorno and the Institute in 1935, "Paris, Capital of the Nineteenth Century", which we'll now look at.

PARIS, CAPITAL OF THE NINETEENTH CENTURY

1. Fourier, or the Arcades

Commercial arteries cut through entire blocks of houses whose owners gain from property speculation. ... How do we experience the regressive and utopian contradiction of these arcades?

Riegl's method is again obvious in Benjamin's attention to the details of ornament, the tactile and optical elements.

Here, in these transitory arcades, even in the fleeting fashions on display in its shops, we find traces of a utopian wish for a completely satisfactory system of *social production*. **Charles Fourier** (1772–1837), the social philosopher, envisaged a bizarre utopia that he named **Harmony**. And where did he imagine his utopian folk would dwell?

2. DAGUERRE, OR THE PANORAMAS

Glass and iron construction, the arcades and the *panoramas* arrive together. Panoramas are painted landscape vistas that unscroll before the spectators: perfect deceptions of day turning to night, moon rises and waterfalls. They introduce the countryside into the city – another utopian image – and point ahead, beyond photography, to cinema.

PHOTOGRAPHY AS A MARKETING AND ADVERTISING DEVICE WILL ENORMOUSLY EXPAND COMMODITY SALES.

Louis-Jacques-Mandé Daguerre (1789–1851), inventor of the **daguerreotype** in 1839, began as a panorama painter.

3. GRANDVILLE, OR THE WORLD EXHIBITIONS

World Exhibitions, begun in London in 1851, are pilgrimages to the commodity phantasmagoria. Commodities are now mass entertainment in which people themselves become commodities. This is the secret behind the art of **Jean Ignace Isidore Gérard Grandville** (1803–47) which ends in his madness. Grandville's illustrated fantasies go to the extremes of utopianism and regression.

UTOPIAN IN EXTENDING THE MODERN~IZING CHARACTER OF THE COMMODITY TO THE UNIVERSE ITSELF.

Grandville stitches the living body to the *inorganic*. Fetishism is indeed "subject to the sex appeal" of inanimate objects. Fashion will then dictate the ritual by which the commodity fetish demands to be worshipped.

4. LOUIS PHILIPPE, OR THE INTERIOR

Not for nothing was Louis Philippe known as the "citizen-king", the epitome of bourgeois domesticity, with his ten children, top hat and rolled umbrella, who mixed freely with Parisians in the streets. With his reign comes the "private person" who must at all costs maintain the illusion of an intimate living space totally separate from the office work space. Hence, the phantasmagorias of the bourgeois interior: the drawing-room as a private box in the world theatre.

THE COLLECTOR IS THE PERFECT OCCUPANT OF THIS INTERIOR UNIVERSE

But occupancy leaves *traces* – and, as in Atget's photographs, there are imprints of *guilty secrets*. **Edgar Allan Poe** (1809–49), who invented the detective story in 1843, captured this eerie quality in his "philosophy of furniture".

5. BAUDELAIRE, OR THE STREETS OF PARIS

The arcade liberates the window-shopper's gaze. Baudelaire portrays this new "man of the crowd", the *flâneur* – the idler; the urban stroller – flip side of the office-hours bourgeois.

The **flâneur** merges with that undomesticated conspirator, the **bohemian artist**, of uncertain economic status.

The bohemian's natural interface is with prostitutes – and death – as we find in Puccini's *La Bohème* (1896). Baudelaire's last poem in *Flowers of Evil*, "The Voyage", ends with the summons, "O Death, old captain, it's time, let's weigh anchor!" But what is his destination? "To the depths of the Unknown, in quest of **something new!**"

6. HAUSSMANN, OR THE BARRICADES

Baron Georges Eugène Haussmann (1809–91), Prefect of the Seine under Napoleon III, called himself "an artist in demolition". To him we owe the Paris we see today, with its great boulevards and long perspectives. He destroyed the working-class areas of the inner city to build his ideal vistas. His real purpose was to prevent the building of barricades, a strategy of the 1848 revolution.

So, despite Haussmann's regressive efforts, an unexpected utopian element creeps back in. Barricades go up again in the Commune uprising of 1871 – and the May Events of 1968 – with plenty of other resistances in between!

TROUBLES WITH THE INSTITUTE

The outline we have just seen – hardly a dozen pages – although useful as a guide, is also misleading. It barely suggests the complex montage of quotation and commentaries that Benjamin's plans would never finalize. This 1936 "blueprint" did initially impress Adorno enough to approach the Institute and plead financial support for Benjamin's "masterpiece" project. Adorno's enthusiasm was soon replaced by another detailed criticism. And so began a see-saw battle, lasting until 1939, with the Institute "money men" over the publication of two scaled-down essays on Baudelaire.

"In the ruins of great buildings, the idea of the plan speaks more impressively than in lesser buildings, however well-preserved they are." Benjamin's own words from the *Trauerspiel* assure us that all is not lost for an interpretation of his arcades project. Virtually all of his crucial works in the 1930s can be understood as pieces out of the unfinishable whole. But by the spring of 1939, Benjamin's life was in grave peril. The Gestapo was seeking his expatriation – evil tidings for a Jew openly active in Communist circles. At their last meeting in January 1938, Benjamin had resisted Adorno's pleas to escape Paris for New York.

Hitler's invasion of Poland, 1 September 1939, followed in two days by France and Britain's allied declaration of war, led to the "precautionary" measure of detention in French internment camps for exiles like Benjamin. Released at the end of November 1939, he returned to Paris.

LAST EXIT ...

Prior to his internment, and just before the outbreak of war, Benjamin had been visited by an emissary from the Institute in New York. Meyer Schapiro, a young art historian, a scholar of Benjamin and Riegl's works, was sent to persuade him to emigrate at once. On the phone, Benjamin suggested a rendezvous at the bistro *Les Deux Magots*. But how would they recognize each other? Benjamin replied, "You'll see." Schapiro and his wife Lillian waited in the bistro ...

Schapiro did not succeed. Why did Benjamin not take this last opportunity to flee? Was it perhaps that he had determined to work on the arcades until the very last moment?

In the winter of 1940, Benjamin undertook his last known writing, "Thesis on the Philosophy of History". These 18 brief aphoristic "Theses" were to serve as provisional theoretical armatures to Baudelaire's central role in the arcades project. But they were also a response to the "new war" in its global synopsis of his generation's entire experience. They were not meant for publication, as Benjamin emphasized in a note to Adorno.

He was right – the "Theses" are among the most often quoted and abused of his writings. Inevitably, too, they remind us of Marx's own "Theses on Feuerbach" (1845), particularly the 11th and last. "The philosophers have only *interpreted* the world in various ways; the point is to *change* it."

SAMPLES FROM THE "THESES"

from Thesis 1. Baron von Kempelen's chess machine was able to play winning games. An automaton puppet in Turkish dress, smoking a hookah pipe, sat playing at a chessboard on a large table. Mirrors cleverly gave the illusion that the table was entirely transparent; but, inside, a little hunchback, expert at chess, guided the puppet's every move.

THE PUPPET CALLED "HISTORICAL MATERIALISM" SHOULD WIN EVERY TIME — IF IT ENLISTS THE SERVICES OF THEOLOGY, WHICH AS WE KNOW TODAY IS SMALL AND UGLY AND MUST KEEP OUT OF SIGHT

from Thesis 9. Klee's "Angelus Novus" again. This is how we can picture the angel of history – his face turned towards the past. Where we see a chain of events, he sees one single catastrophe piling wreckage upon wreckage at his feet.

TIME RUNS OUT ...

France collapses in the Nazi Blitzkrieg of May-June 1940. The Germans occupy Paris on 14 June; the Gestapo seize Benjamin's apartment. The only escape left is to head south and cross the Pyrenees into Spain. But before he goes, Benjamin entrusts his arcade notes to a librarian at the Bibliothèque Nationale: **Georges Bataille** (1897–1962), dissident Surrealist, anti-philosopher and eroticist.

Benjamin, with other refugees, did manage to cross the Spanish border and reach the coastal town of Portbou. But the Spanish government had suddenly revoked all transit visas that might have got him to Lisbon and eventually to safety in America. Refugees were to be sent back to France the next day. Despairing, in ill health and mortally fatigued, Benjamin swallowed an overdose of morphine tablets that night. The official date of his death on the Portbou register is 26 September 1940. He was 48 years of age. His possessions were handed over to a Spanish court on 5 October 1940.

IN TRANSIT

We are left to wonder if Benjamin ever meant to leave Europe. He would remain "in transit", as perhaps he implies in a letter to Adorno, October 1938. "… every now and then, I glance at the city plan of New York that Brecht's son Stefan has mounted on his wall and I walk up and down the long street on the Hudson where your house is."

Something irreplaceable in European culture died with Walter Benjamin. Not the brilliance of a mind only, but a unique spirit, the passionate rescuer of a history in danger of extinction.

What does the critic truly seek? "Contemporary relevance", as Benjamin announced in his plan for the abortive journal, *Angelus Novus*, in 1922. "… according to a legend in the Talmud, the angels – who are born anew every instant in countless numbers – are created in order to perish and to vanish into the void, once they have sung their hymn in the presence of God."

True to his nature as an allegorist critic, Benjamin is a ruin. But what a ruin! "In the spirit of allegory, it is conceived from the outset as a ruin, a fragment. Others may shine resplendently as on the first day; this form preserves the image of beauty to the very last."

FURTHER READING

Works by Walter Benjamin in English Translation

Charles Baudelaire: A Lyric Poet in the Era of High Capitalism, trans. Harry Zohn (London: New Left Books, 1973). Includes: "The Paris of the Second Empire in Baudelaire", "Some Motifs in Baudelaire", "Paris, the Capital of the Nineteenth Century".

Illuminations, ed. Hannah Arendt, trans. Harry Zohn (New York: Harcourt, Brace & World, 1968; London: Collins/Fontana, 1973). Includes: "Unpacking My Library", "The Task of the Translator", "The Storyteller", "Franz Kafka", "Max Brod's Book on Kafka", "What is Epic Theatre?", "On Some Motifs in Baudelaire", "The Image of Proust", "The Work of Art in the Age of Mechanical Reproduction", "Theses on the Philosophy of History".

Moscow Diary, pref. Gershom Scholem, trans. Richard Sieburth, ed. Gary Smith (Cambridge, MA: Harvard University Press, 1986). Supplemented by "Russian Toys", "Preface to a planned series for *Humanité*", letters to Gershom Scholem, Jula Radt, Siegfried Kracauer, Martin Buber and Hugo von Hofmannsthal.

Reflections: Essays, Aphorisms, Autobiographical Writings, ed. Peter Demetz, trans. Edmund Jephcott (New York and London: Harcourt Brace Jovanovich, 1978). Includes: "A Berlin Chronicle", "One-Way Street (selection)", "Moscow", "Marseilles", "Hashish in Marseilles", "Paris, Capital of the Nineteenth Century", "Naples", "Surrealism", "Brecht's *Threepenny Novel*", "Conversations with Brecht", "The Author as Producer", "Karl Kraus", "Critique of Violence", "The Destructive Character", "Fate and Character", "Theologico-Political Fragment", "On Language as Such and on the Language of Man", "On the Mimetic Faculty".

One-Way Street and Other Writings, trans. Edmund Jephcott and Kingsley Shorter (London: New Left Books, 1979). Identical with *Reflections*, except for "Small History of Photography" and "Eduard Fuchs, Collector and Historian".

Understanding Brecht, trans. Anna Bostock (London: New Left Books, 1973). Includes: "What is Epic Theatre?" (first version), "What is Epic Theatre?", "Studies for a Theory of Epic Theatre", "From the Brecht Commentary", "A Family Drama in the Epic Theatre", "The Country where it is Forbidden to Mention the Proletariat", "Commentaries on Poems by Brecht", "Brecht's *Threepenny Novel*", "The Author as Producer", "Conversations with Brecht".

The Origin of German Tragic Drama, trans. John Osborne (London: New Left Books, 1977).

Walter Benjamin, Selected Writings, Volume 1, 1913-1926, ed. Marcus Bullock and Michael W. Jennings (Cambridge, MA and London: The Belknap Press of Harvard University Press, 1996). This contains a wealth of hitherto unpublished material.

Works on Walter Benjamin

The reception of Benjamin's work has vindicated his own insight into the ways in which the optic of the present continually transforms the past. Through its selective focus, which often favours particular texts or phases of Benjamin's authorship to the neglect of others, it constantly reshuffles the internal organization of Benjamin's work. This is most apparent in the categories the reception falls into, listed below.

1. Art Criticism
The Theory of the Avant-Garde, Peter Bürger (Minneapolis: Minnesota University Press, 1984).
On the Museum's Ruins, Douglas Crimp (Cambridge, MA: MIT Press, 1993).
"Gordon Matta Clarke", in *Rock My Religion*, Dan Graham (Cambridge, MA: MIT Press, 1993).
"The Originality of the Avant-Garde", in *The Originality of the Avant-Garde and Other Modernist Myths*, Rosalind Krauss (Cambridge, MA: MIT Press, 1984).
"Towards a Theory of Postmodernism: The Allegorical Impulse", Craig Owens, in *October*, no. 12, Spring 1980.

2. Architectural and Urban Criticism
Architecture and the Text, Jennifer Bloomer (New Haven, CT: Yale University Press, 1993).
The City of Collective Memory, Christine M. Boyer (Cambridge, MA: MIT Press, 1994).
Privacy and Publicity, Beatriz Colomina (Cambridge, MA: MIT Press, 1993).
Benjamin's Passages, Pierre Missac (Cambridge, MA: MIT Press, 1995).

The Dialectics of Seeing: Walter Benjamin and The Arcades Project, Susan Buck-Morss (Cambridge, MA: MIT Press, 1989).
"Walter Benjamin's City Portraits", Peter Szondi, in Gary Smith ed., *On Walter Benjamin* (Cambridge, MA: MIT Press, 1988).
Architecture and Utopia, Manfredo Tafuri (Cambridge, MA: MIT Press, 1976).

3. Philosophy
Aesthetic Theory, Theodor W. Adorno (London: Routledge, 1984).
Walter Benjamin's Philosophy: Destruction and Experience, ed. Andrew Benjamin and Peter Osborne (London: Routledge, 1994).
Walter Benjamin: The Colour of Experience, Howard Caygill (London: Routledge, 1997).
The Melancholy Science: An Introduction to the Thought of Theodor W. Adorno, Gillian Rose (Basingstoke: Macmillan, 1981).

4. Literary Criticism
"Conclusions on Walter Benjamin's 'The Task of the Translator'", Paul de Man, in *Yale French Studies*, no. 69, 1985.
The Dissimulating Harmony, Carol Jacobs (Baltimore: Johns Hopkins University Press, 1978).
Dialectical Images: Walter Benjamin's Theory of Literary Criticism, Michael W. Jennings (Ithaca: Cornell University Press, 1987).

5. Marxism
Romanticism and Marxism, Marcus Bullock (New York: Peter Lang, 1987).
Walter Benjamin, or Towards a Revolutionary Criticism, Terry Eagleton (London: Verso and New Left Books, 1981).
"Walter Benjamin, or, Nostalgia", Frederic Jameson, in *Marxism and Form: Twentieth Century Dialectical Theories of Literature* (Princeton: Princeton University Press, 1971).

Biographies of Walter Benjamin

"A Portrait of Walter Benjamin", Theodor W. Adorno, in *Prisms* (Cambridge, MA: MIT Press, 1981).
"Introduction. Walter Benjamin, 1892-1940", Hannah Arendt, in *Illuminations*, trans. Harry Zohn (New York: Harcourt, Brace & World, 1968; London: Collins/Fontana, 1973).
Walter Benjamin: A Biography, Momme Broderson (London: Verso Press, 1996).
The Story of a Friendship, Gershom Scholem (London: Faber and Faber, 1982).

ACKNOWLEDGEMENTS

Alex Coles would like to thank Mrs N.G. and Mr J.R. Coles. His contribution is dedicated to Alexia.

Andrzej Klimowski wishes to thank Dom Klimowski, Natalia Klimowska and Danusia Schejbal for their invaluable help in designing the book.

THE AUTHORS

Howard Caygill is Professor of Cultural History at Goldsmiths College, University of London. He is the author of *The Art of Judgement* (1989), *A Kant Dictionary* (1995) and *Walter Benjamin: The Colour of Experience* (1997).

Alex Coles is founding editor of *de-, dis-, ex-.*, and an occasional contributor to *Art & Text*. He is currently undertaking PhD research at Goldsmiths College, where he is also a visiting lecturer.

Andrzej Klimowski is an award-winning designer and illustrator, the author of the acclaimed graphic novel, *The Depository*, and a lecturer at the Royal College of Art. He is also the illustrator of *Picasso for Beginners* and *Introducing Kant*.

Richard Appignanesi is the author of *Introducing Postmodernism*, *Freud* and *Lenin and the Russian Revolution*. He is a writer and publisher, and is the originating editor of Icon's *Introducing* series.

Typesetting by **Nancy White**
Speech bubble design by **Dom Klimowski**

Index